UNCOMMON SUCCESS

EVERETT OFORI-ATTA

*Breaking out of
the Matrix of common failure*

Uncommon Success

Uncommon Success

ISBN: 978-1-291-90119-1
Copyright © 2018 by Everett Ofori-Atta
Published in United Kingdom by
PROPHET EVERETT MINISTRIES.

All rights reserved. No portion of this book may be used without the written permission of the publisher, with the exception of brief excerpts in magazine articles, reviews, etc.

For further information or permission, write:
PROPHET EVERETT MINISTRIES
55 Kettering Court
4 Brigstock Road
Thornton Heath
London. CR7 8SR.

www.OforiAtta.com
email: UncommonSuccess@OforiAtta.com
Tel: +44 (0) 208 133 4191

Table of Contents

Introduction	5
Chapter 1 - The Blessing Factor	9
Chapter 2 - A By-Product Of Right Thinking	14
Chapter 3 - Say What You See	18
Chapter 4 - Talk Is Cheap	22
Chapter 5 - The Principal Law of Purpose	28
Chapter 6 - Discovery Of Purpose	39
Chapter 7 - The Righteousness of Faith	48
Chapter 8 - The Word of God	55
Chapter 9 - In Prayer	60
Chapter 10 - First Deal With Sin	65

Introduction

There's an easy way to live life and enjoy it. There's a way to keep a happy smile on your face perpetually. Success shouldn't always be attached to sweat and tears. What testimony is it if you also sweat to succeed like everybody else? There are too many common people...your success should be so outstanding it makes you stand out and you become uncommon. I'm very excited about this book.

Information is vital to every man's success. You can't own what you don't know. The reason so many people have resigned to failure is because they don't know success. Information is the bedrock for all formations. If you're not informed, you cannot be formed and if you're not formed, then you will be deformed. I'm documenting this book so I can contribute information to your life but this might be the one thing that will set you up from deformation.

A middle aged family man was diagnosed of cancer and given six weeks to live. He decided to "set his house in order", trying to make up with everyone he had offended. He even took his family on holiday and all of that. He was beginning to shrink under the influence of the cancer. He was dying!

A miracle however happened. The day before the six weeks he had been given was to expire he had a call from his doctor to say it was all a mistake. The cancerous test result wasn't his result. The question here is, what was it that was killing this man slowly since he wasn't cancerous after all? Information!

The information in your mind is what causes the circumstances in your life. If your mind is wired wrong don't expect your life to be wired right. God cannot do anything against your mind. Your level of thinking is your level of living. A man with the right kind of information is unstoppable. It's important that you wire your mind with the right kind of information.

In the first year of his reign I Daniel understood by books.... (Daniel 9:2)

Uncommon Success

Books are the principal tools for creating an outstanding life. Leaders are readers. Your access to uncommon success is via uncommon books. Understanding will make you outstanding. I pray that the Holy Spirit will work on your mental faculties and grant you uncommon understanding for an uncommon success.

If your future is going to be any different from what you have right now, it will be determined by two things: the friends you keep and the books you read. I heard someone saying the other day, show me your friend and I will show you your character. Apostle Paul also said, "Evil communications corrupt good manners." To be honest with you, your accomplishment will be determined by those who accompany you. Allow me to accompany you into your accomplishment through this book.

God is not taking chances with you. He has invested too much in you to let you go to waste. Your future is glorious. The seed you sow determines the harvest you reap. Along the pages of this book are seeds and nuggets that will grant you an abundant harvest of success.

Uncommon Success

As you read "Uncommon Success", an uncommon harvest will be created in your life. Jesus said,

"Now the parable is this: The seed is the word of God." (Luke 8:11).

Blessed is he that readeth.... (Revelation 1:3)

Chapter One

1

The Blessing Factor

Get ready to be rich! You have a divine promise. A mandate.

The blessing of the LORD makes one rich, And He adds no sorrow with it. (Proverbs 10:22)

There's only one destination for anyone who carries a blessing. You have no other option. You have to end up RICH! The blessing of The Lord doesn't make one poor it makes one rich. That's a good place to shout! You have a divine mandate, a statement of backing, an authorisation (that's what a blessing is — a statement of approval) to make you as rich as your mind can imagine.

Uncommon Success

Get ready!

Riches are your divine heritage. I don't think I have to explain what I mean by the word rich. Let's not over-spiritualise it. Rich means rich. Rich means you have more than you can spend. Your daily income is more than your expenditure. That's rich....and that's your destiny.

If you're not there yet then there's something you ought to do. Let God bless you indeed. Isn't that what Jabez prayed for in 1 Chronicles 4:9-10? "Oh that thou wouldest bless me indeed..." God didn't call you and bless you to be poor. An oath of poverty is not scriptural. As long as you remain poor, God is disappointed. Your destiny is disappointed. Posterity is disappointed. Even if not for yourself (because selfishness is not of God) thousands and thousands of people can do with you being richer than poorer.

For the sake of my brethren and companions, I will now say, "Peace (which is "shalom" in Hebrew, means prosperity, riches, deliverance, etc) be within you." (Psalms 122:8)

Uncommon Success

Many people have been limited by their poor understanding of God. He seems to many to be an uncaring God. What God actually wants to do therefore is prove to all around you that He's able to take care of His own. Your prosperity is more of a testimony than anything you can tell any unsaved person. We've talked and talked as a church, it's time to let our riches talk for us.

People keep asking me how I make it. That to me is more of an opportunity to share my God than any evangelism drive. I have no apologies for the blessing that's making me rich. You know what, I haven't even started. I saw in God that His blessing gives me capacity to become as rich as I can ever want. Since then, there's no stopping me. I'm not enriching myself, God is enriching me. You have any questions, go to God. He destined us for riches. What can we do about it?

One of these days, all the richest people in the world will be products of the church. Very soon! Some of us will not rest until that becomes a reality. I pray that you, my reader, will be one of them in Jesus' name.

I have found out that God wants you rich even more than you want yourself. It's not greed to want to be rich, God Himself wants you even richer. He's able to do exceedingly above whatever you think. Ephesians 3:20. This is not a case of indulgence. The good news is that the poor can hope to become rich. That's the simple truth. If the gospel is not exciting, you haven't heard the true gospel.

When God called me to preach, I was reluctant. Since God doesn't force anyone He had to show me the blessing part. That excited me. My God! That's how I became eager to answer the call.

God is not using blessing, however, as a bait to get people to His side. He just doesn't want anyone in poverty. He didn't make you for that. Living outside of God is what makes some people poor. However, that desire to be rich never leaves man. The pagans, the unbelievers always chase after riches as a sign that the desire God put there is still there.

"Therefore do not worry, saying, 'What shall we eat?' or 'What shall we drink?' or 'What shall we wear?' For after all these things the

Gentiles seek. For your heavenly Father knows that you need all these things. (Matthew 6:31, 32)

They're seeking it, so when you have it….guess what….they will come to you. The gates of hell will not prevail against you. That's church!

You will become a praise in the earth! Your testimony will resound! I prophesy in the name of the Lord Jesus Christ, you have entered into your season of abundant riches. Receive grace to prevail in this season!

Chapter Two

2

A By-Product Of Right Thinking

Success is not an end-product. It's a by-product. The main product is the kingdom of heaven. The Kingdom-of-heaven lifestyle is what God intends for all His children. Jesus came preaching the kingdom. The kingdom was at hand then. "From that time Jesus began to preach and to say, 'Repent, for the kingdom of heaven is at hand.'" (Matthew 4:17). And since the days of John the Baptist until now, the Kingdom of heaven suffers violence and the violent take it by force. Matthew 11:12.

Through your new birth you've taken the kingdom by force. When you became born again you gained access into the kingdom. The kingdom is now within you. Luke 17:21. Then, it was at hand but now, it's within you. Nothing is impossible to you as a believer. Kings are meant to rule and exercise dominion. To have the kingdom within you means you have the ability to rule within you.

The kingdom within gives you the mind of Christ. This is a gift from God. All you need to do to excel now is to exercise your gift, your mind.

Therefore I remind you to stir up the gift of God which is in you through the laying on of my hands. For God has not given us a spirit of fear, but of power and of love and of a sound mind. (II Timothy 1:6, 7)

For "who has known the mind of the LORD that he may instruct Him?" But we have the mind of Christ. (I Corinthians 2:16)

Whatever your mind can think your hand can handle. If it wasn't too big for your mind to think it, it's not too big for your hand to hold it.

Exercise your gift, think big! Your mind is the channel through which the kingdom within you expresses itself. Allow your mind to work. It's the factory ground for the kingdom.

Many people have limited themselves through wrong thinking. Without your mind God can do nothing. "But without thy mind would I do nothing...." (Philemon 1:14). It's very important that you watch your thoughts. Feed your mind with great thoughts. Create a picture of the future you desire and let your mind think on these things. It's so powerful that Proverbs 23:7 says whatsoever you think in your heart, you are. You think poor? You're poor! You think rich? You're rich! You think disease? No wonder you're never well. You think God is The Lord that healeth thee? You're healed! Praise The Lord!

The thing is you can force your mind to think something. Your mind is not a body on its own, it's *your* mind. It's part of you so you can and must control it. Make it think right thoughts. Don't allow it to wander all day long. Surround yourself with things that will give you creative ideas. For example, you don't need as many pictures of yourself from years ago or even months ago or even days ago as you need pictures of what and where you want to be in future hanging around your home. The future is more important than the past even if it's yesterday.

Get a picture of your dream home and hang in a place in your present home where you can't avoid seeing it. When it becomes supernaturally imposed on your mind, the spirit within you will make it possible. In your mind, see yourself making it in life and you are bound to make it.

What do you see...?

Chapter Three

3

Say What You See

Moreover the word of the LORD came to me, saying, "Jeremiah, what do you see?" And I said, "I see a branch of an almond tree." Then the LORD said to me, "You have seen well, for I am ready to perform My word." (Jeremiah 1:11, 12)

Before you experience anything supernatural, you need to say what you see. Have a daily confession of what you see in your mind's eye. Your mouth is the highest authority on this earth. Whatever you call any situation that will be it's name. When you speak, every force under the sun is empowered to do what you say. Your ability to communicate is the strongest muscle on your body. Your mouth can put an end to anything in your life without you lifting a finger.

Let your tongue loose. It holds the key to the fulfilment of every will of God for you. Until you say it you won't see it. You are today what you said yesterday and you will be tomorrow what you say today. There are angels all around you, ready to do your bidding. "Do not let your mouth cause your flesh to sin, nor say before the messenger (angel) of God that it was an error. Why should God be angry at your excuse and destroy the work of your hands?" (Ecclesiastes 5:6)

Your hands are too weak to hold on to riches. Your legs are not fast enough to run after them either. Your mouth on the other hand has all it takes to create the exact environment that fosters prosperity and riches. Say with me, "I am rich!"

This may seem insignificant or lame but saying "I am rich" has set in motion every force on earth to bring your riches to you. A ship, as huge as it is, is controlled by a tiny rudder. That little thing is able to turn the entire ship to the left or to the right. That's what happened when you said "I am rich". You've turned your entire life towards riches.

Look also at ships: although they are so large and are driven by fierce winds, they are turned by a very small rudder wherever the pilot desires. Even so the tongue is a little member and boasts great things. See how great a forest a little fire kindles! (James 3:4, 5)

Say with me again, "I am rich!"

That wide expanse of poverty in your life is being replaced with mansions in your Father's house. I see you living in your own mansion!

If only you can say.... Giant problems, long standing afflictions, curses and evil spells will move if you simply say so. They've all been waiting for you to speak.

For assuredly, I say to you, whoever says to this mountain, 'Be removed and be cast into the sea,' and does not doubt in his heart, but believes that those things he says will be done, he will have whatever he says. (Mark 11:23)

Say something to that situation. Say "I can never be poor! Poverty, OUT of my life!" You might be thinking right now, "Sir, you don't know how hard I work and how broke I still am". Yes. Poverty is a very stubborn spirit. It doesn't move just because you're hardworking. To break the back of poverty you need to say something to poverty. Tell that spirit to move and be cast into the sea and as long as you don't doubt in your heart, it will move.

Chapter Four

4

Talk Is Cheap

I'm aware there are a whole lot of Christians who talk and still have nothing to show for it. There are some who spend hours and hours in prayer speaking to their situation. Most prayer warriors are woeful failures. It's all because talk is cheap.

He told us not to doubt in your heart. We hear people making big confessions but how do we know if they do not doubt in their heart? How do we know if we ourselves are not doubting in our hearts? It is possible to believe in your mind but doubt in your heart. So how do we deal with this?

Corresponding action!

Let your actions prove the weight of your words. You're surrounded by a cloud of witnesses. They're watching to see if you truly believe you're rich. Take steps that show you believe what you said.

How do rich people act? Where do they go and what do they read? Begin to do exactly that. You're not faking it. It's really not about what people think. It's for the cloud of witnesses to see your heart. Start reading business reports and investment bulletins. Start supporting charities and attending wealth seminars. That's what rich people do. You said you're rich and you don't doubt in your heart. To God and to the cloud of witnesses many people just make proud boasts when they say, "I am rich, I am rich!". Their actions are weighed against their words and found empty.

"Talk no more so very proudly; Let no arrogance come from your mouth, For the

LORD is the God of knowledge; And by Him actions are weighed. (I Samuel 2:3)

God is looking for action because action proves your heart. It is your heart that forms your lifestyle. When you believe something in your heart it shows in your lifestyle. Your lifestyle will change when you truly believe something in your heart. Many people are living the same old life because nothing has changed in their heart.

It's one thing to understand the truth and another thing to believe it in your heart. Many times, the facts are not in agreement with the truth. The fact is you're broke and can't pay your bills but the truth is you're rich. When that happens, you will look weird if you begin to believe the truth. Those around you will think you've gone crazy. Your actions will contradict your factual reality.

The Seed Of Faith

This is what I've practiced and taught in my ministry for a long time. I've seen many financial miracles by simply practicing what I call the seed of faith. It's difficult to know what you believe in your heart. But the seed of faith proves it most of the time.

If you can't sacrifice on something you "believe", you don't believe it. A lady, a nurse, who was on the verge of losing her job believed when we told her she's in charge of her situation. She can choose if she wants to give up the job or keep it. She chose to keep it. She took action by sowing a seed of £18.44 a month (this is in our ministry a seed of dominion based on Psalm 18:44). Her boss was fired in the first two months.

I spoke about financial miracles on our radio programme and another lady who was so broke she couldn't even afford to buy fuel for her car the previous day believed. She called in to the programme and pledged to sow an action seed of £44. This is according to Genesis 1, God spoke light on the first day but on the fourth day He created the lights. This sets in motion the law of activation. Four is the prophetic number for ACTION. After making the phone call pledge she checked her online bank account and there was a deposit of £2,000 which she doesn't know where it came from even till today.

God will surprise you today!

I believe in the seed of faith with all my heart. God doesn't need your money, He needs your heart and because many people have their hearts in their money, the seed of faith moves God more than any other act of faith. Sow a seed of faith today and see God move in your affairs like never before.

My son, give me your heart, And let your eyes observe my ways. (Proverbs 23:26)

"He asked for my heart", you might say, "So why is money being involved in this?" Well, I read in the scripture how that my treasure (or money) is connected to my heart.

For where your treasure is, there your heart will be also. (Matthew 6:21)

God's heart is in His kingdom work on earth. When you sow your seed of faith into the work of the Kingdom, you show where your heart truly is. God blesses us and enriches us because

Uncommon Success

of the work of the Kingdom on earth. He taught us to even pray that the Kingdom will come so whatever you do to expand and extend the Kingdom gets God's attention like nothing else. You're next in line for a financial miracle. Receive it in Jesus' name!

Chapter Five

5

The Principal Law of Purpose

When the purpose of a thing is not known abuse is inevitable. Think about it. Using a toothbrush as a paint brush makes it look useless. It's a brush but it's not for painting. You can call it useless and throw it in a bin but that doesn't make it useless because no matter what you do you won't be able to use a paint brush to clean your teeth either.

Every product has its own proper purpose. You are a product. God made you for a specific purpose. This is why we believe evolution and atheism is a plot of the enemy to destroy humanity. People live and die like animals these days. If you don't discover your purpose you will abuse your life and some people might actually even find you useless. However, you're very useful to your Maker. There's a reason why He is still keeping you here alive. If you discover your purpose, it will become even more imperative that He keeps you alive. Every product has a purpose.

I shall not die, but live, and declare the works of the Lord. (Psalms 118:17)

Your life was not an afterthought. He had a specific purpose in mind before manufacturing you. Your parents may not think so but that's why they are parents and not creators. Your Creator God used them as vessels to carry you into the world. They may have tried to abort you thinking you were a mistake but you're here to fulfill destiny. It doesn't matter how old you are now, it's never too late to discover and fulfill your purpose. That discovery will lead to a recovery of the wasted years. You will no longer be stressed or depressed, you will only make progress. Halleluiah!

Every product will find its proper purpose by referring to its manufacturer. You are a product. If your purpose is not already obvious make reference to your Manufacturer. He still has His original intentions for your life intact. Don't abuse your life. Uncommon success is a result of uncommon discoveries.

The book of Genesis is not an attempt at recounting history but a revelation that enables humanity to reinstate destiny. I went through Genesis and I came out with some amazing findings by the Holy Ghost. I discovered that a relationship with the Creator is the first step into success. I'm not talking about a casual relationship with God. All some people have to show for their relationship with God is a sanctimonious "piousity".

Discover God as your Creator.

In the beginning God created.... (Genesis 1:1).

To know God as Creator is the beginning of uncommon success. To begin life on a successful note, you need to know the God who created in the beginning. If He created you then

Uncommon Success

He has a purpose in mind for you. Seek Him as your Creator. The Word of God is not a historical account for intellectual satisfaction but a manual for success. It is the Creator's manual for the successful operation of this complex product called man.

Every discovery in the Word leads to a recovery of destiny. Uncommon success is only a result of uncommon encounters in the uncommon "book of the law". This is not another religious holy book. He will reveal to you all the information relevant to your specific purpose if only you will determine to know Him as your Maker and search the Manual tirelessly.

This book of the law shall not depart out of thy mouth; but thou shalt meditate therein day and night, that thou mayest observe to do according to all that is written therein: for then thou shalt make thy way prosperous, and then thou shalt have good success. (Joshua 1:8)

The reason many live purposelessly is because of their lack of understanding of the Manual for success.

In The Old Testament:

In Genesis, He is the Creator God.

In Exodus, He is the Redeemer.

In Leviticus, He is your sanctification.

In Numbers, He is your guide.

In Deuteronomy, He is your teacher.

In Joshua, He is the mighty conqueror,

In Judges, He gives victory over enemies.

In Ruth, He is your kinsman, your lover, your redeemer.

In I Samuel, He is the root of Jesse.

In 2 Samuel, He is the Son of David.

In 1 Kings and 2 Kings, He is King of Kings and Lord of Lords.

Uncommon Success

In 1st and 2nd Chronicles, He is your intercessor and High Priest.

In Ezra, He is your temple, your house of worship.

In Nehemiah, He is your mighty wall, protecting you from your enemies.

In Esther, He stands in the gap to deliver you from your enemies.

In Job, He is the arbitrator who not only understands your struggles, but has the power to do something about them.

In Psalms, He is your song–and your reason to sing.

In Proverbs, He is your wisdom, helping you make sense of life and live it successfully.

In Ecclesiastes, He is your purpose, delivering you from vanity..

In the Song of Solomon, He is your lover, your Rose of Sharon.

In Isaiah, He is the mighty counselor, the prince of peace, the everlasting father, and more. He's everything you need.

In Jeremiah, He is your balm of Gilead, the soothing salve for your sin-sick soul.

In Lamentations, He is the ever-faithful one upon whom you can depend.

In Ezekiel, He is your wheel in the middle of a wheel–the one who assures that dry, dead bones will come alive again.

In Daniel, He is the ancient of days, the everlasting God who never runs out of time.

In Hosea, He is your faithful lover, always beckoning you to come back–even when you have abandoned Him.

In Joel, He is your refuge, keeping you safe in times of trouble.

In Amos, He is the husbandman, the one you can depend on to stay by your side.

In Obadiah, He is Lord of the Kingdom.

In Jonah, He is your salvation, bringing you back within His will.

In Micah, He is judge of the nation.

In Nahum, He is the jealous God.

In Habakkuk, He is the Holy One.

In Zephaniah, He is the witness.

In Haggai, He overthrows the enemies.

In Zechariah, He is Lord of Hosts.

In Malachi, He is the messenger of the covenant.

In the New Testament:

In Matthew, He is king of the Jews.

In Mark, He is the servant.

In Luke, He is the Son of Man, feeling what you feel.

Uncommon Success

In John, He is the Son of God.

In Acts, He is Saviour of the world.

In Romans, He is the righteousness of God.

In I Corinthians, He is the rock that followed Israel.

In II Corinthians, He the triumphant one, giving victory.

In Galatians, He is your liberty; He sets you free.

In Ephesians, He is head of the Church.

In Philippians, He is your joy.

In Colossians, He is your completeness.

In I Thessalonians, He is your hope.

In II Thessalonians, He is your glory.

In I Timothy, He is your faith.

In II Timothy, He is your stability.

Uncommon Success

In Titus He is your reason for serving.

In Philemon, He is your benefactor.

In Hebrews, He is your perfection.

In James, He is the power behind your faith.

In I Peter, He is your example.

In II Peter, He is your purity.

In I John, He is your life.

In II John, He is your pattern.

In III John, He is your motivation.

In Jude, He is the foundation of your faith.

In Revelation, He is your coming King.

Every detail of scripture is of utmost importance and necessary for your success. Knowing Him as Creator will lead you into knowing Him as Redeemer. Complete and sustained redemption and deliverance is a result of a discovery of purpose. When you know what you're about in life, the enemy can't toy with you.

Uncommon Success

God said to Moses to tell Pharaoh to let "My People" go! Their purpose as a nation was to be God's showpiece nation. God called them My People. Their purpose was well defined and that produced their unconditional redemption. As you're reading now, God is calling someone, "My Servant", "My International Businessman/Businesswoman" or even "My Showpiece Millionaire". May your purpose be uncovered in Jesus' mighty name!

Chapter Six

6

Discovery Of Purpose

How can purpose be discovered? If that's your question, you've asked a good question. There are two very important things every individual must do with their purpose: Discover it and pursue it. Let me answer your question and then I'll talk about the next aspect which is pursuit.

If you must discover your purpose you must follow the leading of The Lord. When God leads, everything follows. The reason many have lost control of their lives is the lack of Divine direction. It's only God who can lead you into your purpose. When God uncovers your destiny, every good thing discovers you.

The problem with a lot of people is that they don't want people to be disappointed in them. They keep following what is not leading them to destiny. Popular opinion is what creates common failures. Where your destiny is might not be popular with people but you need to follow God's leading. It is better to disappoint a man than disappoint your destiny.

He found him in a desert land, and in the waste howling wilderness; **he led him about**, *he instructed him, he kept him as the apple of his eye.* (Deuteronomy 32:10)

The nation of Israel was peculiar because they were led by God. From a waste howling wilderness, he led them into a land flowing with milk and honey. They had cheap victory over all opposition as they went from one nation to another. He suffered no one to do them wrong saying, "Touch not mine anointed and do my prophets no harm". (Psalm 105:13-15).

The Red sea saw them and fled. Jordan was also driven aback. The mountains were skipping like rams and the hills like lambs. (Psalm 114:1-4).

When God leads, miracles are an everyday event. The supernatural becomes natural.

Desire to be led. What you don't desire you don't deserve.

There's no aspect of your life that does not require His leading. Every step along your destiny's path is very important. Don't leave any of it to chance. Allow God to lead every step of the way.

Many people decide to do it their own way because they can't trust God. How can they trust God? They can't even see Him. Cursed is everyone, however, who puts their trust in the arm of flesh. God does not punish people, He polishes people. Everything God tells you is to improve your life. God is a good God. Trust Him!

Many years ago when The Lord uncovered my destiny as a preacher it wasn't popular with my immediate circle of relations. Many of my friends and family thought I was making a mistake. Someone even asked me, "how did you hear God?" As if those who hear God have a different set of ears from what we all have. I was rejected and opposed to say the least. Anything I attempted was crushed by people who felt they knew the will of God for my life.

It's amazing! Today, what I enjoy would never have been possible without me following God's instruction. My heart is always on fire anytime I have to do anything related to my area of calling. Nobody can compete with me in this area. Howbeit, if I had settled for a common destiny I would have been struggling to catch up with those whose area of calling that is. I had to obey God rather than man.

Don't settle for nursing when God's choice for you is music. You may not know in clear terms where to place your next step but follow God. From where you are, you can begin to be successful. Success is not a finished product, it is a journey which begins with discovering purpose. Begin to be successful today.

Let me show you a few things that point to your purpose in life just in case you're not too sure what God has for you. God speaks to you through these things.

Three Pointers To Purpose

1. **Natural Talent**. The things you have a natural edge on, point to your purpose in life. There are some things you are able to do easily and without as much stress as others. Oprah Winfrey is a natural talker. She has gone on to become one successful talk show host. Can you imagine such a person as an accountant? She would have failed woefully.

What is an agriculturalist doing as a politician? What is a trader doing as a medical doctor? Watch your natural abilities and channel your efforts into developing and making use of them. Every product is naturally designed to fulfil its purpose. A product that will be used for cutting will naturally have a sharp edge somewhere. The reason you are so different is because your purpose is unique. You're not strange, you're unique!

I will not speak too much about natural talent because God doesn't necessarily use you in what you're capable of doing. In my natural self I'm very introverted. You should meet me at home to know this about me. Many of my contemporaries are extroverted as preachers. They speak as they're thinking. On my part, I take longer to process my speech in my mind. I'm not naturally cut out for preaching but when the Holy Ghost comes upon me, I walk in fire, I tread on serpents and scorpions and I humiliate the devil like no man's business. Natural talent has nothing to do with my calling so I will talk about the next pointer.

2. **Spiritual Gifts**. As you spend time in God's presence, certain abilities develop which were not naturally there. The Spirit is able to use you in a particular area more than in another area. This is a huge pointer to your purpose. Apostle Paul asks believers to covet earnestly the best gifts. (1 Corinthians 12:31). What is "best" to me may not be best to someone else. It's important you spend time in His presence worshipping and praying so your spiritual gifts will be exposed.

As a young Christian, I was completely consumed with excitement when I saw successful preachers. I was always awed by the ministry of preachers. I say this because ministry is not limited to preaching. When a man discovers his area of calling in life, whether a farmer, doctor or preacher, he is said to be in ministry. The ministry of preachers excited me more than anything a doctor or a multi-million businessman would do. I wasn't sure then if God had called me to preach but my excitement was unparalleled. I coveted that gift with all my being. To me that was the best gift.

No wonder it became obvious that God had called me to the preaching ministry. Not everyone will inspire you. A trainee plumber cannot be apprenticed to a carpenter. Their "gifts" are different. When you encounter people who carry what you carry, the "baby in you" will leap.

And it came to pass, that, when Elisabeth heard the salutation of Mary, the babe leaped in her womb; and Elisabeth was filled with the Holy Ghost. (Luke 1:41)

The reason certain pages of the Bible make more sense to you than others is because of the nature of your purpose in life. Your spiritual make-up is what attracts you to those areas. Develop it. It points to your purpose in life.

3. **God's Special Voice**. The third pointer to your purpose is the voice of God in your life. God gives you visions and dreams as He utters His special voice to you. He confirms His Word to you. Follow His voice.

Your ears shall hear a word behind you, saying, "This is the way, walk in it," Whenever you turn to the right hand Or whenever you turn to the left. (Isaiah 30:21)

Actually, I should say His voice is following you. Listen! God will speak to you about where you actually belong. Let me state here that this is most likely to happen to someone who is on the move and involved in something not an idle person. Don't sit and wait for God to speak to you about what to do. Do something. You will hear His voice behind you (your ears shall hear a word behind you....) not before you.

The reason many seem never to hear His voice is because of idleness. Jesus called His disciples to be Apostles whiles they were busy fishing. Fishing wasn't their calling so He redirected them to save them from frustration. Be involved in something while you listen for God's voice in directing your next step.

Take God's voice as a steering wheel. The effect of a steering wheel on a car is not felt until the car is in motion. You make the move, acknowledge Him and then He will direct your path.
In all your ways acknowledge Him, And He shall direct your paths. (Proverbs 3:6)

I hope this settles you. Many people are waiting to hear His voice before they move yet all those God has spoken to concerning their various areas of expertise and exploits have a record of already being on the move. You will hear His voice clearly from today!

Chapter Seven

7

The Righteousness of Faith

For therein is the righteousness of God revealed from faith to faith: as it is written, The just shall live by faith. (Romans 1:17 KJV).

Faith is the instrument for justifiable living. A lot of people have no right living. When you hear someone say "no one knows tomorrow" you know there's no faith. Everyone who has faith knows that tomorrow can only get better. Life is rooted in God and faith is our ONLY access to God. Without God, there's no hope in this life so you're reduced to living by chance.

This is why David could say "I shall NOT die, but live..." (Psalm 118:17). He was confident!

God has a reason to keep you here. When you discover God's purpose for your life, you walk in faith. It might look like nothing is happening but faith makes you hold on and you can say "because He lives I can face tomorrow", "I know my redeemer lives" (Job 19:25).

That's what is called faith. Job was so deep in faith that he could say "though He slay me, yet will I trust Him..." (Job 13:15). He knew his trouble and affliction didn't have power over his life. Life is enjoyable when one is locked into faith. Refuse to endure life, you must enjoy life.

Faith is a tangible substance. Hebrews 11:1 says, "Faith is the SUBSTANCE of things hoped for..." That means there's a substance inside hope. Hope is only imaginary but that substance that pops out of hope is called faith. When a person is walking in hope nobody might know but faith is a substance, it cannot go unnoticed. Faith changes the look of a person. It changes the face, the eyes, the talk and the walk.

Jesus told His disciples to HAVE faith in God (Mark 11:22). Faith is something to have. Just like you have a shirt, you have a shoe, you can have faith. Faith is tangible! Faith is not abstract. Paul also said, "Above all, TAKING the shield of faith..." Take it! Pick it up like you pick up your house or car keys. Faith is not just positive thinking.

The day you get faith the enemy will know it. You will have an identity in the spirit. Changes will take place when no physical effort had been applied. What causes those changes is that tangible faith you have taken.

When the enemy sees a person of faith he sees a different kind of man - a superman. He's terrified. He cannot stand you. Before you command, he's already begging for leniency. Too many people try to make an impression on people but the enemy is not impressed. When you have faith though, you don't try to impress people. God becomes your only focus and the devil comes under attack whenever you come on the scene.

I see a generation of people who will terrorise the camp of the devil. These people have faith. They have an identity in heaven. Their names are written in the Lamb's Book of Life.

Notwithstanding in this rejoice not, that the spirits are subject unto you; but rather rejoice, because your names are written in heaven. (Luke 10:20).

What caused their names to be written in heaven? Faith. Heaven is God's home and for your name to get to heaven you must have gotten God's attention. And the Bible says, "...without faith it is impossible to please Him." (Hebrews 11:6). It's impossible to get God's attention without faith. Faith is the most attractive thing to God. God is excited when you have faith. That's what makes you look like Him. That's His image! God is a faith God so you need to be a faith child.

A lot of people think of God as impossible to please. He's like an angry headmaster ready to smash them with His rod and staff. The devil has clouded their understanding and made them see the Word of God as a book of condemnation filled with "thou shalt nots". But you see, faith comes by hearing the Word. If you're antagonistic to the Word how can you ever have faith? How can you ever please God?

So then faith cometh by hearing, and hearing by the word of God. (Romans 10:17).

Faith comes by hearing and hearing. You won't want to hear and hear again when you're not excited about it. I have some books that I keep reading over and over again. I never get tired of them. Every time I pick them up, I'm excited. For some Christians, even when the preacher is preaching they already know what he's going to say so there's no expectation for anything new. No excitement.

When you're able to hear, hear and hear again, you're able to get into a relationship with the Spirit of that Word. It's no longer the principles you know in your head but the Spirit you know in your heart. Spirit calls unto spirit. Deep calls unto deep. (Psalm 42:7). Smith Wigglesworth once said, "A library will swell your head but the Bible will enlarge your heart."

Get excited about the Word. You will never be righteous without a deep and unquenchable love for the Word. I'm not talking about religious commitment though. Forty-five minutes of the Word on Sunday morning is not enough. There are precious nuggets hidden inside the Word and only committed searchers find it. God is not looking to condemn you, He's looking to empower you. He's looking to enthrone you. He's actually looking to enrich you!

Many people who are putting on a robe of poverty think they're rather putting on a robe of righteousness. Poverty is not synonymous with righteousness. In fact, righteous sounds more like riches. Hallelujah! I tear that robe of poverty to pieces! God wants you rich; spirit, soul and body! When you truly connect with God, the devil can't put poverty on you. The Word will enrich you.

Beloved, I wish above all things that thou mayest prosper and be in health, even as thy soul prospereth. (3 John 1:2).

Anytime I ask The Lord to show me a way to prosper in a particular area of life, the first thing

Uncommon Success

He does is to show me His Word. One time, God told me to write books and to publish His Word. He showed me, "The Lord gave the word: great was the company of those that published it." (Psalms 68:11). And then He said, "I will bless those who read your books". He showed me, "Blessed is he that readeth..." (Revelation 1:3).

You cannot go wrong with the Word. If all you see in the Word is "Thou shalt nots", ask Him to show you something else. There's more to the Word of God. He deals with sin, imputes righteousness and ushers you into prosperity and uncommon success all through His Word.

Chapter Eight

8

The Word of God

The Word is like Fire

Is not my word like as a fire? saith the Lord ; and like a hammer that breaketh the rock in pieces? (Jeremiah 23:29)

Fire is used to purify gold. When gold has not gone through fire, it looks like dirt, worthless. The fire of the Word purifies the believer. It consumes negativity. It purifies your environment and makes your real worth emerge. Too many things are clouding your actual destiny. Allow the fire to consume them.

When you stick to the Word some friends will leave you. People who don't qualify to go with you into your destiny will be put in their rightful place. Sometimes it's painful when people you think are worthy begin to abandon you. Don't cry over such people. You are the gold and they are the impurities that need to drop off. Your friend determines your end. Thank God, friendship is not by force, friendship is by choice. Choose friends who love your commitment to the Word and let the Word work. Your altar must constantly have fire. "The fire shall ever be burning upon the altar; it shall never go out." (Leviticus 6:13).

The fire is the Word. The altar is the place of sacrifice or your service to God. When there's fire, flies (who represent demons) will be kept away. The sacrifice (which was raw meat in the Old Testament) on its own attracts flies. Isn't that why so many believers today have their lives become a safe haven for demons? Their sacrifice or service to God has attracted enemies. They didn't have so much trouble when they were not saved. Of course, at that time they didn't have an altar neither did they have a sacrifice to attract flies.

Keep the fire burning. God wants you hot, not lukewarm. A preacher who serves God without Word-fire makes more enemies than converts.

God wants you on fire because He's a consuming fire Himself. (Hebrews 12:29).

The Word Is God

Whenever you enter trouble, increase the temperature! Get more Word. It's not time to cry. That's not the time to say, "Oh Lord, where are you?" "Oh Lord, why me?" You should know where He is. He is in His Word. "In the beginning was the Word, and the Word was with God, and the Word was God." (John 1:1). Without the Word, nothing will get done. Without the Word, nothing will change.

I will worship toward thy holy temple, and praise thy name for thy lovingkindness and for thy truth: ***for thou hast magnified thy word above all thy name.*** (Psalms 138:2).

Stop shouting "Lord, Lord, Lord" "Jesus, Jesus, Jesus". He has magnified His Word above His name. He has more respect for His Word than He has for all His Name. ""You shall not take the name of the Lord your God in vain (meaning empty, non-substantiated noise), for the Lord will not hold him guiltless who takes His name in vain. (Exodus 20:7, bracketed comment mine).

The devil is not cast out because you're shouting "Jesus, Jesus". The devil is cast out because the Word said it. "And these signs will follow those who believe: In My name they will cast out demons; they will speak with new tongues." (Mark 16:17). "In My name" doesn't mean you're shouting His name. It only means you're doing it in His stead, you're doing it for Him, just as He would have done it if He were here...in His name.

He was clothed with a robe dipped in blood, and His name is called The Word of God. (Revelation 19:13).

Did you see that? His Name is called The Word of God. Some people take the name "Jesus" like "abracadabra" - a magic word. This is funny. Some years ago I had a Portuguese housemate called Jesus so I learnt to identify the one I'm talking to in my prayer. I didn't want my housemate to come responding to my prayer in case he overheard me. The power of the name is in the Word. Go for the Word.

God is bound by what He says. His integrity forbids Him from breaking His own Word and once He notices you with His Word, He imputes righteousness on you.

Chapter Nine

9

In Prayer

It is a principle and a law in the spirit that anyone who is involved in prayer must qualify for breakthrough. Prayer is for answering; the result of prayer is answers. In Jeremiah 33:3 The Lord says "Call to Me, and I will answer you, and show you great and mighty things, which you do not know." Your duty is to call, His duty is to answer.

Examples abound in scripture where God answered prayer. Men like us prayed, and God committed Himself to answer them. In other words, God had been waiting to hear a prayer so

He could answer. He answers prayer, that's what He does. Where there is no prayer, He has nothing to answer. God is attracted to prayer. Praying people have the exclusive privilege of God's attention.

Abraham prayed. God had been waiting to hear his prayer so He can answer.

So Abraham prayed to God; and God healed Abimelech, his wife, and his female servants. Then they bore children. (Genesis 20:17)

God's ear is inclined to the voice of those who call upon Him. Abraham's prayer triggered the end of barrenness in the life of Abimelech and his family. God has an answer to your prayer if you will pray. It's a condition. Do you desire to experience great and mighty things? Pray! He will show you great and mighty things.

Nothing is too great or too mighty for a praying believer. Your problem is not too big. To men it may be big but God is not intimidated. Just pray!

Now Isaac pleaded with the Lord for his wife, because she was barren; and the Lord granted his plea, and Rebekah his wife conceived. (Genesis 25:21)

Isaac was not a superman. He only operated the principle which says, "once there's a prayer, there's an answer". It's a principle. The Lord will grant you your own plea today! I am prophesying to you...that age long predicament has an end and I declare that the end is now! In Jesus' mighty name!

You've worried enough. You've talked to everyone about the problem except God. "Be anxious for nothing, but in everything by prayer and supplication, with thanksgiving, let your requests be made known to God." (Philippians 4:6). You don't have a peculiar problem, you only have a peculiar silence! Have the audacity to disrupt that silence. Pray! God is as real as the people you're discussing your problem with. Talk to God! Speak to Him! He's a prayer answering God.

I've been in the prophetic ministry since 1998 and I've recorded so many notable miracles. This is not to say I've accomplished but that God is faithful and I trust Him to do same in your life. You will step higher. I've seen the sick healed by the power of prayer. You will be healed! I've seen mighty deliverances. I've seen mental disorders healed and delivered. There's nothing God cannot do. Get set! We're going on an exciting journey of breakthroughs. In Jesus' mighty name!

In 2001, I met with a lady who had been pregnant 14 months. While in prayer with her, The Lord showed me she had an aunt and gave me her name who was also pregnant and that she was a fetish priestess. She confirmed that her aunt was also pregnant and well overdue. I prayed with her, broke the curse that was over the family and gave her a point of contact according to the Word of The Lord and that night she delivered just at midnight. The baby was one unique bouncing baby girl. A week later her aunt also delivered and renounced the fetish. Praise God!

Your miracle is next! This book shall be your point of contact. I'm praying for all my readers now. The demonic oppression is shattered today in Jesus' mighty name!

There are some who pray for the religious excitement of it. I don't believe in that. Five minutes of prayer should have five minutes of answers. Prayer is communication with God; talking to and hearing from God. Your prayer must be answered. Your God is not dumb.

Chapter Ten

10

First Deal With Sin

Sin Sinks; Sin Stinks! If you don't deal with it, sin will make you sink.

Righteousness exalts a nation, But sin is a reproach to any people. (Proverbs 14:34)

Sin brings shame. Sin brings reproach. In the long run, sin is not fun anymore. The reason why many people keep sinking in life is because they keep sinning in life. Deal with every hidden sin. Destroy sin and its effect - reproach. Reproach is another word for disgrace or shame. There are many who have been disgraced today as a result of sin.

The destruction sin causes is enormous. It's so deceptive, the sinner often feels it's the best and only thing to do and yet it destroys. We give ourselves many excuses as to why we can't do without sin. The guy is going down in life but he blames everything and everyone except the real culprit. Sin causes blindness. You will stand next to your blessing and call it a curse. The few people I have encountered who don't like me only do what they do because of sin. I challenge people to stand for righteousness wherever I go. The righteous fall seven times and rise up again but the sinner will fall into mischief. Rise up!

I hate poverty; I hate disease; but I believe it is even more imperative that we hate sin. Sin brings disease and poverty. Now, what you like, you never lack. What you respect, you will attract. I pray we will respect holiness and eschew sin. I declare a spirit of holiness on you today! To enter into the fullness of God's provision, we need to love what He loves and hate what He hates. There's nothing God hates more than sin.

Behold, the Lord's hand is not shortened, That it cannot save; Nor His ear heavy, That it cannot hear. But your iniquities have separated you from your God; And your sins have hidden His face from you, So that He will not hear. (Isaiah 59:1-2)

God cannot behold sin. I don't know why we claim to be His children and don't treat sin with the same level of contempt. It's a weakness the devil encourages. He would rather we were not so serious about dealing with sin.

Now, you may be asking, can we live without sin? Many people give themselves excuses in this area. The Bible says, if we say we have no sin we deceive ourselves; all have sinned. All those excuses won't help us. Some say, "Even Paul struggled with sin". Well, he did. "For the good that I will to do, I do not do; but the evil I will not to do, that I practice. (Romans 7:19)". So here's my question: do we now assume that God doesn't know our state?

For He knows our frame; He remembers that we are dust. (Psalms 103:14).

And yet, Jesus told this lady caught in adultery to "go and sin no more".

*She said, "No one, Lord." And Jesus said to her, "Neither do I condemn you; **go and sin no more.**"* (John 8:11)

He knows your state too well and also knows that you can live without sin. You are what God says you are. Don't consider yourself to be what your experiences tell you that you are. Every destined child of God walks by expectation and not by experience. Expect to be what God says you are.

Sin Is Rooted In Unbelief

Many times what we consider to be sin is not the same thing God considers sin at all. Some religious Christians judge people by the law they see them breaking. They make themselves "spiritual police officers" ready to convict anyone they catch breaking the law. Holiness does not always mean "abiding by the law".

In Matthew 19:16-22, a young man came to Jesus and wanted to find out how he could live a life of power (eternal life). Jesus asked him to obey the commandments but this guy had the audacity to say before God that he had always obeyed the law. It was true but it was hypocritical because this guy was law abiding only when people were seeing him. Obviously, he couldn't have been caught in sin. You just wouldn't find him breaking the law but in His heart he always broke the two greatest commandments, "You shall love the Lord your God...,' and 'love your neighbour as yourself." (Luke 10:27).

When Jesus asked him to demonstrate his love for his neighbour by selling his belongings and giving to the poor and and also demonstrate his love for God by following Him, the Bible says he went away sad. This guy didn't believe God could be his Jehovah Jireh Provider and because of that he broke the greatest commandments.

A lot of people continue to live in sin because of unbelief. Unbelief is sin in itself. When God sees a man who's living in sin, all He sees is unbelief. If that unbelief could be dealt with, God would gladly impute righteousness. He did it for Abraham, He'll do it for you. Did Abraham live in sinless perfection? No. He slept with his maid and drove her away from his house with his little teenaged boy. "Such wickedness!" But he believed in God. If there's anything we must deal with, it's unbelief.

Beware, brethren, lest there be in any of you an evil heart of unbelief in departing from the living God. (Hebrews 3:12)

God sees unbelief as an EVIL HEART. It turns Him off! We may be seeing fornication or stealing or lying but God sees unbelief. All the manifestations of sin stem from the evil heart of unbelief. Out of the abundance of the heart the mouth speaks. We only see a manifestation of the unseen. An evil heart results in an evil person (even if he appears to be very law abiding) and a clean heart results in a holy person (even if people catch him or her breaking one law or the other).

Afterward Jesus found him in the temple, and said to him, "See, you have been made well. Sin no more, lest a worse thing come upon you." (John 5:14)

The only thing that can get the devil to strike again after a person has been delivered and healed is sin but that sin is actually unbelief.

Without faith it is impossible to please God and maintain His presence and without His presence all devils are welcome with no inhibitions. God is attracted to faith like an ant is to sugar. On the other hand, unbelief is the worst form of evil before The Lord. Unbelief repels God. Whenever a man is left blank through unbelief, the demon returns with seven more wicked spirits so no matter how powerful the original healing was, a worse thing comes upon the person. Sin no more, saith The Lord!

Sin sinks; sin stinks! If sin is not dealt with, it will sink the believer.

Now, welcome to this new life of faith and righteousness! All your prayers are being answered today! You're set for a life of Uncommon Success!

You need to receive Jesus into your life as your Lord and personal Saviour. He will forgive and cleanse you of all your sins. Pray this:

Lord, my Father, I come to you today acknowledging my sin and inadequacy. I ask for forgiveness and cleansing by the blood of Jesus. I believe Jesus died for me and rose again on the third day for me. I receive Him into my life today to be my Lord and personal Saviour. I choose to follow You and Serve You with my life. I renounce satan and every work of flesh and the pleasures of this world to embrace your perfect will for me which is eternal joy, peace and righteousness. Thank you for saving me today, my life is never the same in Jesus' name!

Amen!

If you have prayed this prayer I would love to hear from you. Leave me an email at papa@oforiatta.com

www.ingramcontent.com/pod-product-compliance
Lightning Source LLC
LaVergne TN
LVHW051709080426
835511LV00017B/2816